At Night, beneath Trees

At Night, beneath Trees Michael Krüger

Selected Poems Translated by Richard Dove

George Braziller New York

"Service Station" first appeared in *The New Yorker*
and "Little German National Anthem" in *The Harvard Review*.
Grateful acknowledgment is made to both these publications.

First published in the United States
by George Braziller, Inc. in 1998

Poems included in this selection
were originally published in Austria
by Residenz Verlag in the following volumes:

Brief Nach Hause © 1993 by Residenz Verlag
Nachts, unter Bäumen © 1996 by Residenz Verlag

English translation © 1998 by Richard Dove

For information, please address the publisher:

George Braziller, Inc.
171 Madison Avenue
New York, New York 10016

Library of Congress Cataloging-in-Publication Data:

Krüger, Michael, 1943–
    [Poems. English. Selections]
    At Night, beneath Trees : selected poems / Michael Krüger ;
translated by Richard Dove.
        p. cm.
    Poems from *Brief Nach Hause* published in 1993
and *Nachts, unter Bäumen* published in 1996.
        ISBN 0-8076-1431-9 (pbk.)
        1. Krüger, Michael, 1943—Translations into English.
I. Dove, Richard, 1954– . II. Title.
PT2671.R736A23   1998
831'.914—dc21   97-39393
                        CIP

Design and Composition by Neko Buildings

Printed and bound in the United States of America

First Edition

Contents

From **Letter Home**
 [Brief nach Hause, 1993]

Guided Tour
 [Führung] *3*

Little German National Anthem
 [Deutschlandliedchen] *4*

The Parrot
 [Der Papagei] *5*

Carbon Paper
 [Durchschlagpapier] *7*

Advice
 [Ratschlag] *8*

Letter
 [Brief] *9*

Service Station
 [Reparaturwerkstätte] *10*

Two Men on a Park Bench
 [Zwei Männer auf der Parkbank] *11*

I Am Weary
 [Ich bin müde] *12*

When the Weather Is Fine
 [Bei klarem Wetter] *13*

Taking a Rest
 [Ausruhen] *14*

Afternoon
 [Nachmittags] *15*

Commemorative Sheet for Günter Eich
[Gedenkblatt für Günter Eich]   *16*

In the Summertime
[Im Sommer]   *17*

PS
[P.S.]   *18*

Letter to a Child
[Brief an ein Kind]   *20*

Letter to Dan Pagis
[Brief an Dan Pagis]   *22*

Letter Home
[Brief nach Hause]   *24*

Returning to an Empty House
[Rückkehr in ein leeres Haus]   *28*

The Day After
[Am Tag danach]   *33*

From **At Night, beneath Trees**
[Nachts, unter Bäumen, 1996]

In Conversation
[Im Gespräch]   *37*

A House
[Ein Haus]   *38*

To Be Continued
[Fortsetzung folgt]   *39*

The Bed
[Das Bett]   *40*

Looking Out into the Garden
[Blick in den Garten]   *41*

Mailshot
[Post] *42*

Wind
[Wind] *43*

The Painter's Allocution
[Rede des Malers] *44*

The Museum Attendant's Allocution
[Rede des Museumswärters] *45*

The Old Woman's Allocution
[Rede der alten Frau] *46*

The Fool's Allocution
[Rede des Narren] *47*

The Translator's Allocution
[Rede des Übersetzers] *48*

Petrarch's Allocution on Descending Mont Ventoux
[Rede des Petrarca nach dem Abstieg vom
Mont Ventoux] *49*

The Mailman's Allocution
[Rede des Postboten] *50*

The Allocution of the Despairing
[Rede des Verzweifelten] *51*

January 13, '95
[13. Januar 1995] *53*

1995/2/1
[Brief vom 1. Februar 1995] *54*

February '95
[Im Februar 1995] *55*

Draft of a Nature Poem
[Entwurf eines Naturgedichts] *56*

Postcard from Budapest, April '95
[Postkarte aus Budapest, April '95] *58*

Summer '95
[Sommer '95]   *59*

Little Scene
[Kleines Bild]   *60*

At Night, beneath Trees
[Nachts, unter Bäumen]   *61*

Photo Album
[Photoalbum]   *62*

Note for the Files
[Aktennotiz]   *63*

Postcard, in Tiny Writing
[Postkarte, in winziger Schrift]   *64*

Laughlin's Secret
[Laughlins Geheimnis]   *66*

Natives
[Eingeborene]   *67*

Up in the Gods, with Hobbes
[Auf der Galerie, mit Hobbes]   *68*

Education
[Erziehung]   *69*

Trompe l'Oeil
[Trompe-l'oeil]   *70*

Episode
[Episode]   *71*

While Dawn Is Cracking
[Sehr früh am Morgen]   *72*

In the Plane, above Europe Still
[Im Flugzeug, noch über Europa]   *73*

In Cologne, Winter
[Köln, im Winter]   *74*

Film
[Film]   *75*

In Memory of Cioran
  [Zur Erinnerung an Cioran]   *76*

Rumor, '95
  [Gerücht 1995]   *77*

The Way They Write
  [Wie sie schreiben]   *78*

Far from Perennial Verses
  [Die kleinen Verse]   *79*

Summer Storm
  [Sommersturm]   *80*

To Zbigniew Herbert
  [An Zbigniew Herbert]   *82*

Writers' Congress
  [Schriftstellerkongreß]   *84*

The Cemetery
  [Der Friedhof]   *86*

Last Day of the Year
  [Der letzte Tag des Jahres]   *89*

from **Letter Home**

[Brief nach Hause, 1993]

Guided Tour

What you see here's been wrested out of History's jaws.
All beams are old; all doorframes too,
in which the dead used to hang, for three days.
At this table, world history was written
(the notches betray as much): here a gallows,
and there the king's head. We can only conjecture
who this woman can be, legs astraddle.
Wars were in fashion because there were still destinies
which had to be fulfilled. There were goals.
A sharp sword came out of his mouth, which meant
he could express himself, be understood:
language had not yet been mastered by Doubt
but was shaped by vision; no sign of an archive
of emptiness. A person at this table received
his identity from the looks of others, under duress too.
There was no chair in this room for Fear,
which is why it nestled down into the painters' fine brushes,
as you can see from these pictures: here it has survived
in a transport of color. The pictures were cleaned
when the last war ended. Although Enlightenment
virtues are still important to us, they're not
absolute. They learned, in those days, to classify birds
into those which one hears and those which one sees. Today we
    listen
to what the town has to tell us about time congestion, lateness.
If you'd be so kind as to follow me, this is the way to the
exit.

Little German National Anthem

Just imagine we owned this house,
the friendly creaking of the stairs
and the mice behind the wainscoting.
Just imagine the shades of those
who lived here once were thronging
the table too, telling stories.
We'd be listening. Wearing their clothes,
with collars turned inside out, dyed in the
wool. And the corpulent angel
of history would be chopping onions,
shedding salty tears for us.

Just imagine we asked the brook
to leave its gravelly bed so the fish
would not have to cross the land
on its way into our pot.
Just imagine that we were sleeping
at night in these beds and that the country
covered us right up with its dreams.

Just imagine we dreamed we had to
leave the house, and had no idea
where we should go.

The Parrot

Don't talk to me of truth,
please don't, in this Museum
of Art. Ask the fly
that's turned that window into a matter
of life and death, making the dirt
dance choice arabesques. The master
has left the house, don't ask
how; the paint is still wet
on the canvas; and, inside the computer,
a short poem's waiting
for its last line.
The guests alone are lolling still
in the easy chairs: worn out, as though gagged,
by a tangled discussion.
Nothing more can be got
beyond: that is the truth.
Talk to the stones outside,
growing dreamily out of the earth,
or else to the clouds, to the rain.
No points of view though, please,
but only sacred signs. I'm
the resident parrot, my word hoard's
as small as that of my master,
whose name escapes me.
I am old.
And, please, no questions! For if there were
an answer, it would be concealed

within the question. My plumage cries
out to be described
but only from outside, through the window,
so that the guests are not woken.

Carbon Paper

In the beginning, I read, there was perhaps the cross
and, above the cross, a pallid sun,
spirited up into the sky as if by magic.
The sky has been written across. Despite
the handiwork of an alien hand,
I can still make out its long-suffering face: two snails for eyes,
and, for a mouth, a fish's skeleton.
I hazily read the unreadable love,
the deception in language: I know, you know—
child's play for even the blind to decipher.

Advice

If you want to paint paradise
looking its best, don't skimp
on color. Too little
smooths everything—for example:
the ocean will look like a notional
ocean. Just paint one tear,
just paint the reflection of your face
in a drop of water,
and there is the wave,
the pebble on the ocean floor,
the shipwreck, paradise itself.
Too little color's too much
for us, and we (after all) want it
to speak our language
in our pictures. We've always
understood what appears:
a house by an ocean
in a hot summer,
entirely white: as though we'd painted
in snow.

Letter

Yesterday evening—don't
ask me why—I went into the village
church and sat down, shivering,
among the old folk
in one of the cramped pews;
I moved my lips as though I'd something
to contribute. It was dead easy.
As soon as the first prayer was over
(we also prayed for you), the mask
of Goodness grew over my face.
Up front, not demanding a solution,
the old priest was pecking listlessly
around in the gospel, like some black bird,
but didn't appear to find
anything that could have allured us.
No saving thread, no consolation.
One hour and everything was over.
Outside, an unexpectedly bright light
played on the lake, and a wind sprang up—
letting me see the under-
surface of the leaves.

Service Station

I'm just repeating the sentences
of those who've spoken before me—public servants, middle
managers, white-collar workers, ordinary mortals.
They all say more or less the same:
my car is sputtering, vibrating wildly,
will not speed up when I put my foot down.
Blindly I grope for words
as though they were a tool. If something is missing,
I am all eyes. I can't help
my language—it's there and has got to be
used or else it will soon be rusty.
I say to my wife: the food tastes fine.
Or else: I love you. Sometimes I fling
myself into the arms of words, but that's
bad for business. Take yesterday:
a poet was here, a real old-timer—
pure gibberish. His spark plugs were all
clogged up with soot, that's all that was wrong,
but he couldn't describe it, too sad.
It is a mistake to believe, he said,
but by then I was under the hood.

Two Men on a Park Bench

We got around a lot while alive,
washing our hands at noon in the ocean,
dipping our eyes in perpetual snow
and driving away the savage beasts
with our laughter (which can still be heard
when the wind has dropped).
Others we got to do our sleeping;
there wasn't a war that was safe from us.
And if our food were to drop from our spoons,
we tossed it over our shoulders.
Good riders, we never dismounted
till we had arrived. When we unstrapped the saddles
our horses decomposed into dust.
O yes, there were enemies everywhere!
We circled round their tracks, collecting
the earth in a pouch made of animal hide,
which then got hung up above the stove.
If the earth was dry, we'd fling the enemy
into the garden. We'd no clear idea
of who we were; there was no time for questions.
The tracks, however, kept closing in,
our breath grew shorter, and so we settled
on this bench. The tracks now run
right through beneath us, and on, and on,
invisible to the naked eye.

I Am Weary

My neighbor is sinking a shaft
into the earth, tired of sun,
of rain, of me. He's building a house
beneath his house, is founding a city
which bears his name. He's designing
a calendar, guarded by
a four-eyed serpent.
Roots are growing up through his dreams,
snails pointing the colorless way.
He stores water in a blackbird's skull bone
and shares his worldly goods with mice.
We rarely meet.
On occasion he sends a raven
up to knock on my window,
a bloody message lodged in its beak.
Between the lines sprout stinging nettles
which move me to tears.
Before I forget to, I read it
and am already asleep. No time
for explanations.

When the Weather Is Fine

Finally, in the morning, the horizon opens:
you're free to see the drowsing sun.
The ancient rolls of gods record one
who represents the augmentation of happiness
by underhand means: I too let myself
be guided by him—go after him, carefree,
across the newly roused grass, passing by
the dead man's straw where the green beetles hang out.
Stories narrate themselves by themselves when the weather
is fine. Go with the wind, the last
storyteller, who's nothing to tell you.

Taking a Rest

A flower's been blooming on the wall since yesterday,
a white star set in glimmering green: it waxes
and wanes before my eyes, then fades away
into the crumbling stone in whose shadow
I am sitting. Poems, rhymed dreams, occur to me,
cleansed now of contingence, their cadence austere
and confidential. Just as one says: You've
seen me, let's go our separate ways.
Alas, my gross eyes: for them the stone
is only a thing, as it doesn't grow, being petrified
at what that could mean for the whole of nature.

Afternoon

Books by the window, thinned by the sun,
behind your back the heavy breathing of the pages:
rising and falling, rising and falling . . .
Apart from novels, poems, each houses
a hidden language, a couple of words
in an arid paper nest; the rest
is lumpy grammar.
At times there's a sentence that all divine.
When questioned, put on the spot, under pressure,
they none of them own up to having heard it.

A friend returns, brings the world
indoors—the mountain that, burning, slid into the ocean,
the birdcalls, the snail's trail left by Doubt.
He tells you of regions like empty classrooms
(all knowledge driven out with a pitchfork).
Hey, come on, you're exaggerating!
But he's already turned to a new page,
is pointing to a watermark, the labyrinth
of a finger from way back, two thumbwidths
from the original.

Salts proliferate on the pages, spawning trees
on whose parched branches lies are thriving.
Have no expectations. Count letters, syllables,
till a word arises which inspires your trust.
That word will get you back into the sentence.

Commemorative Sheet for Günter Eich

Out in the garden stand two shoes,
not a pair, out of breath
after traveling far.
They look both old and bold
in the dewy grass of dawn.
One is squeaking in prose,
the other in stumbling verse.
We have invented roads for ourselves
which no man ever set
foot upon . . . It's pretty bombastic,
not all that credible and, after all:
a good shoe doesn't betray the path
which it has taken,
a good shoe stays silent.
I really could chuck them away
but leave them. Nearer noon
they've upped and left.

In the Summertime

A bat is scrawling away on the water,
a dog's sprawled godforsaken in the dust.
What does that leave? A string of days,
bright, open, light, remote. Something's weighing
down on my throat, and what's in my throat is
no frog, for sure. And in my eye there's a hand
which is writing: night shade, undecided.

PS

for Marianne and Peter

Yesterday there were stewed apples made of fruit from Tutzing,
fruit which we had (as it were) known from birth:
we had already admired the blossom, its bright
shriek in spring, and later the tiny green balls
and the way the grass turned white in the wake of the storm.
We watched away as the apples grew bigger,
got covered with stains but still stayed green,
stayed greenish-black. Back in the summer we wondered
how they'd taste in the fall,
and when the first ones lay in the grass, green set off by green,
we threw them across the garden for the dogs to chase,
for Billie and Ella. For many years now
we've been counting on the apples from the garden in Tutzing.
While the world (whatever that is) demands
we assume the relativity of all forms of knowledge,
while we're left with understanding, unable to see our way
through anything anymore, the apple tree's lesson is simple:
it gets repeated year after year in an old-fashioned manner
regardless of what people think of each other,
and shows a certitude that Reason can only dream of.
Shortly after the frost—the front had moved to the west—
we picked the apples, which now looked ancient,
diseased and decrepit, as they ought to.
They tasted exceptionally good, somewhat sour,
and after the first bite we had to pause.
Then yesterday came what was left over, stewed.

While eating we had a lengthy discussion
about the fact that we have to assume a reality
to which to react, one way or another.
I can't say we were over the moon.

Letter to a Child

for Simon

Thank you warmly for your letter.
The fresh green of the envelope pleased me—
I'm going to keep it, although I too wish to part with
things. I'll have to die when this place is full.
Your envelope's attached to the lamp:
it's darker now, the paper is no longer white,
and your handwriting's gleaming: I'll never again
forget my name or address. There's too much
of everything—we've got to learn
to throw things away. The question is: what?
Tears come to my eyes when I pass the garbage can
in the morning. Yesterday, beneath coffee grounds
and potato peel, a whole coat was lying there, one sleeve hang-
ing over the edge, one button short.
A proper coat, a coat people wear.
Everything turns into history, trash, if a button's missing—
a laughable button made of plastic.
The massive Soviet Union has just fallen
apart, and nobody knows what the parts are called,
but each part has a name. Fine names
that make the newscaster on TV—the man
with the round face—stutter. All men are brothers now,
but otherwise nothing has changed. I'm sorry, there's too much
    now,
too little *yesterday* and *tomorrow* in this letter; all's
gathered up in this *now*, this point
which closes something. I'm not sure if I can muster

a lion. ("Lion" is spelled with an "i," by the way—
regards to your teacher.) At any rate,
the lion that lives here is looking for another apartment.
It brings me the mail, from time to time, in its dripping mouth,
which means I can't work out who's the sender.
I'll only write to you in future anyway. Visit me soon,
for when you're grown up I'll already be
dead.

Letter to Dan Pagis

Dear friend, the enemy's disappeared.
He left behind a note, brown paper:
"You're not to remember, at any price."
At times, when I'm sitting in the chair
that you sat in and the cloud's lucent map
is laying out a worm-eaten shadow
on the road, I see the horse,
the gravedigger's horse, and remember the time
we exchanged our words: my name
is Adam and this is Abel, my good-natured son;
don't let his behavior put you off.
We've booked a ticket right to the very
end of the world, can stop over as often
as we like. There'll always be a garden, a house,
a child that dreams of wind from the ocean,
of fire in the fields. It isn't good
to sit for too long . . . We used to live
in that house over there; it was a shed
for the goats. There were still many gods in those days.
And many tongues crowded desperately
around few words. No end was in sight.
And next-to-no bureaucracy. My dad, who was bright,
applied himself to reading the symptoms
because he was crazy enough to want to abolish disease.
Since he died, we've been traveling,
escorted by voice and text, our shadows.

This, dear Dan Pagis, is what we wanted to translate—
transport, word by word, to the other language.
Can it be me that's sitting in your chair?

Letter Home

You ask what I'm doing here. "Nothing"
would be a lie: I'm reading too much in too many
books which bewilder me or leave me
cold, and I'm worrying more and more that they
won't make good all this grief (does that sound
too pompous?). What I mean is: the more I grasp
(or think I grasp), the greater my fear,
which subsides into grief.
Are these only words now, inhabited briefly,
to be moved out of at short—at no—notice
because they signify nothing to us? I just can't buy
the collected despairs these philosophers peddle,
I hate them for their presumptuousness
in the face of a darkening creation:
"there's nothing left to see that's worth looking at"
stared at me recently from a blind book
whose author's holding lectures at three places at once
on the lack of authentic experience:
an image, it states, always falsifies our expectation.
Which must mean an image that we can't see.
I'm standing, though, in this expectation's freezing shadow
and feel fear turning my brain to ice.
Cold hat, you'll say.
Now it is History's turn to be dumped.
For instance, I was reading a book
by a Japanese American on
"The End of History." Not much to write home about

as regards the deductions it makes, *au fond*
nothing new, I've already forgotten
the author's name. And yet this tome
really makes me see red—the arrogant way,
the unanguished way, he bids farewell
and approves this farewell as though he were
proclaiming some truth. For isn't all
that we were and that we could become
wedged between two farewells. So there must
be a time to bid farewell to the end
of history too, to self-consciousness.
And on whose behalf is this author speaking?
That of the Africans dying like dirt in their salty deserts?
Or that of thirty merry philosophers of history
who'll now have to switch to economics?
No one knows any longer whom they're speaking to—
could this perhaps be the true end of history?
Everyone smilingly climbs on board a given discourse
and lets the *zeitgeist* rock them a bit
so there is some movement. The whole thing's a fragment,
a snatch of delusion, a stubbed toe in the march of ideas.
(I urinated my name into the snow outside
the house yesterday—there was just enough:
I felt a childish compulsion to read
my name once again!) In the room next to mine
a Scottish brain physiologist has pitched his tent
(Aharon Eisenschitz, "a good old Scottish
name"); "as a Jew and a scientist"
he could die laughing about my despairs.
If these philosophical gentlemen would care to look
through a microscope, he said yesterday,
they'd see that there cannot be an end.

He drinks dark beer and smokes like a chimney
to cure his cough. If, say, one group
of cells is behind the perceptual content
"end of history," there's bound to be
another group that is gunning for
the future of the thing in question—
if we assume that consciousness
consists of some 100 billion nerve cells
in the brain. The question is: what cells
govern what? And what cells govern
the desperation, the racking pain, that's
stalking my head? He laughs and then tells me stories,
punctuated by laughter, about the electric goings-on
in the visual cortex of cats, though he's personally
frightened of cats.
At any rate, they're about to give the world up as lost
if they view the situation we're in
as the end of history—that's the way
the Scottish commander of the neuronal regiments sees it.
I walk a lot, downstream around noon
where, in summer, the moles' metropolis stands.
The obdurate snouts of the dwarf pines poke
out of the snow and grimly report
on "Life down under." It's so quiet down there
that you think you can hear the animals breathing.
And then, on the other side of the brook
whose wan blue water is gasping for air,
I walk back upstream, with the end of history
lodged in my mind—as wafer-thin as a host
and as crumbly as these walls which,
dismayed, are giving in to the snow. Yes,
something is ending, something is out to capitulate

this winter—a couple of the cells
which dwelt for millennia on beginning,
on ways, on light, on longing, on promise,
are now worn out. And yet . . . I've also
written a poem, deaf to reason,
"Returning to an Empty House"—I'm enclosing it.
You won't perhaps find it poetic enough.
"The tempest raised a veil of purest white" was
how it was meant to start, but it jibbed at
that kind of diction. Otherwise: not very much
to report. When I'm troubled, I tell myself
"We will see, we'll see all right,"
but I fear in the end we will get to see
nothing.

Returning to an Empty House

You didn't remember to water the flowers,
and an apple's dry mummy is stiff in the
ashtray, a mournful brown wreck in a field
of ash. There are hairs all round too, as if some
poor creature had met a foul end. On the windowsill
flies, their legs in the air, and a spider which moves
away like a dead weight when I touch it.
It's all spilt milk, with a coating of dust.
No image. That corpse they found in the Alps, 4,000
years old, an image of man, still had hair
when they sighted it under the ice, and a smile
on its lips, the first known smile, in all
likelihood, in the brief little history
of mankind—and from it derives the whole
fine art of being human. At some point
it came apart like the cloud that's coming apart now
outside the window: not some sudden severance
but rather a gentle unraveling, a fluffy parting
with each part promising to keep
a tiny scrap of the other for ever.
One part of this ancient smile is allied
with man whenever, unsure of himself,
he stumbles over a threshold, the other
has grown into an inordinate laugh that no
longer fits into any face. Since that time, a smile's
been hiding in every guffaw, and vice versa too—
the law holds true in this empty house.

Everything's turning up again, coming back to light,
now the snow is melting, a tooth
for a tooth. And even the handful of pitiful words
which are still straightforwardly ours, and which
we squirreled away till spring so we'd find
a rhyme for meadows and sheep and light's
rite, are becoming apparent, sodden like
dogdirt and forming a lusterless wreath round themselves,
from which they then shyly arise: grace,
return. All things are on hand, all things,
including departure, demise; it's just that they don't
look the same when someone suddenly pulls
away the blanket of dross and dream, releasing a smile
which ascends like a bird alarmed in its sleep.
The tempest raised a veil of purest white . . .
The earth, sick unto death, sweats out its dead
and stops the future becoming the future.
Plates in the sink. Dried coffee grounds
are narrating stories in my favor with both beginnings
and endings, as though I'd only a past.
No sleep between the lines, no respite,
no death which kills us with sharp-edged eyes.
I've got to sit down, my head is swimming
with all the invocations booming out of this silence,
out of the silence of silence, out of the navel of language
down under the snow. Things are appearing
outside the house: stones, ferns, the brown grass
and, there in their midst, old forgotten tracks that
showed the way long before the road did, the much-trodden
path. And behind lies the wood which barely harbors
the roe deer's bounding shadows until
they're engulfed by the dark. And no

trails, so all is in order in this empty
house. You've forgotten, lost to whatever, to turn
the computer off too: I can see its glassy
emerald eye, the other light. It now knows music
back to front, can simulate every single note
with its AAA1 memory. All things are
on hand. All things fit easily onto a chip
the size of a thumbnail—words and notes,
the whole of history, and when the eye's burning
all things are with us, simultaneous,
with or without us. It all works without us,
nobody's looking for us now. Each delicate smile
and each guffaw from time out of mind
has access to me. All things allow us
to share in them, and we share in all.
The whispering tissue of traces which go to make
consciousness, history, a tenuous
present, is centered on one point,
the point of irreversible beauty,
which now is slowly fading. When was I
last in this house?
I move from photo to photo; all strangers.
One was a thinker, I recognize him:
there's death in his eyes, the death which loved him
from cradle to grave. They're all hanging here to be
forgotten. Look, there's the idiot, the family idiot,
destroyer of books: his folks couldn't work out
whether he was in the grips of madness
or just adept at the language of madness;
there's the dear lived-in face he was wont to
press to the ground to hear the moles
at work. Human beings become more mournful

the longer they hang here behind cobwebs, glass.
They look like children grown old overnight,
like children without a future. And then
these newspapers, printed nature. History
is over, it's said, there's nothing to
look forward to. We've got to live on
what we have and are, no new growth is in the cards,
no new installment of dreams. And no art.
So that was it: from the ban on incest
right down to free-market economics we swept
the board. With skirts getting longer and shorter by turns,
and somewhere along the way the invention of perspective,
the twelve-tone series, the cordless phone.
Of course at some point the king's head had to
roll, and time was ripe at another juncture
for universal suffrage. We can still recall
the circling finger in the sand, and chalk,
and pencil, and typewriter. And the historians
will hit upon whether Landor wrote
with his right or his left hand. History will win
at the end of history—the history of the
handkerchief that wiped tears for good
from the face of the earth. And everything just
in our heads, in which several wires are better
or differently linked than in those of dogs.
I envy dogs. I'd like to embrace
every horse. Every bird turns my head, every crow.
So now we are to take our leave from this
empty house, from these lofty looks,
these lordly gestures, our humble words,
an impossible present. Having struggled
up from our squatting position we walked a few yards erect,

straight ahead, invented the gods and quickly
forgot them again, and now it's all over.
A drag mark, transparent, is running through
the house, across paper, like that made by snails.
And yet . . . I am reaching no conclusion, no
beginning. Not much mail. One fellow wants money,
another's sent poems. One is a tactful description of
an empty house in which you can walk from room to room
without let or hindrance, wall or door.
The house is empty. A good sort of poem
in free verse, so useless and so detestably
true.

The Day After

In fact, what I aimed to do today (Monday)
was get to write a love poem of sorts,
an unassuming piece on a couple
I kept my eyes on yesterday
in a pub (called Kosta). I wasn't out,
à la Dante, "to imitate God's language,"
nor to resort to irony, but just to describe
the nexus of power, desire, and knowledge,
as revealed to yours truly, your typical
nervous observer: in snatches of speech,
looks, attitudes, in the manner in which
the man ordered more wine, the woman smoked.
A love poem was to have emerged
which didn't breathe a word about
the steady dissolution of culture—
the thing which preoccupies me all day
because its progress cannot be checked.
Inquiring into the nature of poetry
challenges us to reflect on the state
of our existence. If one doesn't study
its mistakes, the mistakes made by poems,
one's bound to repeat them; it's no good either
invoking Freedom, which (it's said)
becomes flesh in poems, even in
their very line breaks. I had in mind
the artless utopia of a happy
meeting of bodies, unmindful of death, destruction

and catastrophe. The words, though,
refused to yield up their truth,
as though they'd no idea how perception
and knowledge are rendered into language.
This may be the reason why love
poems are so short these days,
and why their findings—if one may say this—
are so foreseeable.

from **At Night, beneath Trees**

[Nachts, unter Bäumen, 1996]

For George Braziller

In Conversation

You know that I'm only a guest
in this house, a man who seeks
the shade beneath the transcendent trees,
a short-lived alliance as evening draws down.
It's me who is the eye while the wind
is reading in the hedge, and painting
a grimace on the back of the brook
which is struggling seaward—to protect it
against the night, which has not yet struck.
Between removal and return
the salt is glittering ambivalently
in the falling sun.
You know whom I turn to:
the face which sees me,
unrecognizing. Day's
done; the watchmen are rising, white,
out of the grass and are sitting in judgment—
but always in such a way that they keep
in God's good books.

A House

The house was asleep already
when we set foot in it,
tired out with our fellows.
Some alien grief was the only thing
watching over the fire;
we were expected.
I tore off the page of the calendar:
it showed the world the way it was.
The body which we don't know
knows the movement
which keeps us together,
apart.

To Be Continued

The house is bristling still with the mousetraps
the last tenant set, and in the corners
stand little dishes flush with red poison—
designed to give the flies one last
fling. Black beetles are out
of it on their backs, as though
they'd been trying their best to tread air.
The only protagonists who seem
at home are the spiders: with flimsy leglets,
they're busy narrating the novel whose outcome
we're unaware of. It started, apparently,
with a murder that left a red thread
on all the walls that hold this place up.
And then the day of the victim dawned, and then came
the war. And now we live here.
Waiting for the wind which will bring
the host of words home from the empty sky.

The Bed

for Ariane

After you'd left
I stripped your bed.
The mattress looked
like a convict, finished.
Now, when I turn out the light,
I can't be sure any more
on which side I'm lying.
With one foot in jail
and the other in freedom,
sleep's out of the question.

Looking Out into the Garden

If only I were able to describe
the fluttering lashes of the laurel—
which rise in the gale and only fall
when the shadows take umbrage from the dark green—
in words, in words which are consonant.
Beauty is not a prerogative
of the person at the window, staring
out at the bordered paths, the well
(whose stones are making off) and the herbs
(arranged in classes, just like in school);
one's privilege is the words that are crouching
restlessly in one as though inside a breathing ark,
just waiting for the rain to stop.
Some of them leave one's mouth prematurely
and fly off in horror, others stay put
inside the husk assigned to them.
We choose our language, and not vice versa,
and even eyes which soundlessly sound off
seek the right words when the time
is ripe. Yet sometimes, when one is standing
silently by the window, watching the laurel
coquettishly yielding to the wind,
a voice which isn't one's own speaks up. Says:
fluttering lashes.

Mailshot

Today, by no means out of the blue, came
notice that we're to be given notice, stamped
on the paper with a fist—which caused the pigeons
under the eaves to start whispering apprehensively. Either
you're out of this house by the end of March. Or else?
God willing. But *you* won't oust *us*.
Too many words are concealed in this house:
you'd only have to open the door and they'd go for you
like famished beasts. This new clause, squire,
enabling landlords to kick tenants out if they claim to
need the property, is an unsecured
credential in this world of ours: you're not the sovereign,
merely the curator, of this out-of-line tomb
of books. We're here to carry on
a conversation, collecting memories
for a specific purpose; our eyes
are of this world, though we have to close them
more and more often to see anything.
What's scandalous is what's visible, and visibly
you're dragging your belly across the garden,
some icy fire in your hand to pour scorn
on poets. You're an automaton,
and no one has found the button that makes you
grind into action. Till March, then, a life
in the gallows' shadow. And just enough time left
to chuck out one's clock.

Wind

A simple universal answer
embracing both grains of sand and stars,
both God and worm. A tool, some forceps:
the instruments needed to measure the world
can only be found in the world. I'm standing
by the window. Below one dog's yapping at another,
plastering him with gurgling sounds. His mistress
is mumbling to herself as she pores over prices
in the jeweler's window display. I can see
her lips moving on the glass:
May a prayer help her. Dear God . . .
Just try to imagine a God
endowed with infinite talent. The second dog's
taking it lying down. Why doesn't he
run away? It's all experience,
and now he could easily make himself scarce. God's only
half human—for ever the same identical answers:
experience is, for Him, a term which has no meaning.
People are moving faster now, as though
some wind were propelling them, some invisible force.
They're all swimming past, all standing still,
and turning their collars up in the teeth of the biting wind
that's taking their sentences with it and turning them
into a simple universal answer.

The Painter's Allocution

I have, like so many before me, made sacrifices
to Beauty. My hand was the priest, an ascetic
locked into a cult of colors. It lived for dark surfaces—
down from bright-gray to bluish-black—and would not suffer
people and things. And in this way, canvas by canvas,
an ashen house got built—for Beauty, who never
herself showed up. Shall I make a new start?
My work is done. The world is asleep
in the cup of my hand and twitches, blind-eyed,
when its dreams are oppressive. My picture is finished.
I won't paint again.

The Museum Attendant's Allocution

I've seen the world
in paintings. (And I've seen myself
in the salt-white eye of the hare
that pleads to live for ever
as death sets in.)
I shared in every single death.

The Old Woman's Allocution

This is where the boat put out; the wind caught it up,
a joy for the eyes, though the water was shallow still.
Jellyfish danced in the boiling surf
in blazing gowns, and the scythe-like complaints
of the seagulls above the metallic water
were siren-sweet. The man at the helm
divided anguish: half on each side.
Only the small guy they called the "philosopher"
('cause he was shortsighted) was allowed to chew
his salt in the middle: good for the bones.
They sailed through the straits where sea becomes sky
and purity part of impurity.
And then the ocean grew calm again.
One man made it. Decorated in the war
before he died.—"In which war was that?"—
In one of the last ones, the old woman said.

The Fool's Allocution

Believe me, I can understand what the birds
are saying: the whistles, the trills, of the nuthatch,
the thrushes' nervous chatter,
the wild refrain of the tawny owl
and the siskin's metallic patter
are not alien to me. When these creatures—
bashful at first and hesitant—
strike up their song of praise in the morning,
counterpointed by the magpies' raucous plaints
and the grating gossip of the crows,
when finches, warblers, buntings and larks
are at choir practice, I catch every word.
The doctors are at a loss.
They can't hear the linnet's command
(the one which shuts down day), can't fathom
the swifts' piercing cries
when they roll summer up to take
south with them. For those with ears, these notes
are signaling: fluting calls and scatterbrained row
attract each other until a sentence comes into being,
a story—complete with a mating call and an admonition—
which takes to the air in feeble September,
some brownish chaff on the sky's
high canvas, not hard to read in the wintertime.

The Translator's Allocution

for Friedhelm Kemp

Over a hundred times now I've
translated the moon, the poets'
friend, and haven't betrayed her.
I've made her melt into italics
or fattened her up with semibold type
when she was waning.
Have also, as best I could,
turned all those sighs—
since they're part of the language orbiting her—
into garrulous time.
Ahs! become her better than Ohs!—
statistically speaking, that is.
*All must be done anew, all
said anew* was my maxim.
I only got paid for one syllable:
moon.
Use only one term
for every concept, advises the head
of the Language Bank: it helps
the world to communicate.
Words are no one's property,
yet cost us dearly in terms of
hard cash. Demand for words rises
in proportion to GDP
so make economies where you can,
just leave it at:
moon.

Petrarch's Allocution
on Descending Mont Ventoux

for Bazon

I didn't see a thing, I only looked.
A huddled horizon of mountains: there it was
before my eyes, an episodic fragment
of all the mountains I have never climbed.
The winding of a river, sliver-thin,
seized my eye, made me follow,
until the white glare swallowed it.
A path, from the east, was toiling its way up,
up to the field of shards sustaining me.
After a long hour standing at the summit
down I came, tired from seeing nothing, happy,
with my Augustine safe in an outer pocket,
dog-ears at every turn. From him I learned
that it is bounds which bring forth boundlessness;
I know, that's nothing at all to do with eyes.
May others after me inspect this mountain
and see what's still left. Not that much at all.

The Mailman's Allocution

I've got a charming collection
of postcards I couldn't deliver.
Arranged in strict alphabetical order.
Vacation greetings, with unctuous
thumbmarks as signatures;
block capitals putting the knife into lovers;
down-to-earth advice: don't forget
to turn off the gas. All the things which link
people. Hands which jauntily squander themselves,
and others that, under the line, are straitlaced.
All those lovely canceled faces:
Adenauer, Franco, the doleful king of Greece
who, although long exiled, was still being
stamped on. Even a pelican
and a tulip grace the collection.
There's one I like particularly:
mailed in New York, it went right round the world
without its message falling on ears of any kind.
It reads: I forgive you.
Like hell.

The Allocution of the Despairing

There's no time left to make up for lost time:
the roads are too poor, the cart too small,
and all that's still with us is what fitted once
into a coat pocket. We sometimes wonder
what it could be: it feels cool and round
like the petrified head of some animal.
Where we now live, lost time would—in any case—
be out of place. In our new apartment
dwells the Present. It's there at table
when we eat; It sweats Its way
through the night in our bed, dreaming
the better part of our dreams;
and when we go to work It crackles
softly between our files. When we finally
open our mouths to tell It what
we think, It speaks for us about Its goals.
When we're not watching, the Present
writes poems, using our pen,
to keep abreast of language. It got
the top prize from the Academy
for Its sonnet "Coldness Is the Future":
"History's a history of temperature."
Nature's aesthetically imperfect,
the poem claims, and grows impoverished, waxes,
mixes, at will. And only the breaking-apart
of stones engenders their individuality.

Properly rhymed. And we, it concludes,
are the lumpy sand by the grave of identity.
Can we be blamed if we think so fondly
of lost time?

January 13, '95

Red rowanberries in the strident snowlight,
and (nearby) sloes, glowing bluish-black
in the winter sun. There's not one green leaf
to detain one's look which, insatiate,
is prowling the boughs. Such constant searching
wears longing down till it's threadbare, shabby—
an ancient winter overcoat
that can't keep you warm.
You hold out your hand, and wait
for the voice which will say what you must:
sloes and snow and rowanberries,
that must suffice. Say after me.

1995/2/1

Many thanks for your recent call.
I was so speechless because my sister
had only just died and, with her,
the gist of the childhood we shared.
It makes you see how little is yours,
and what's left doesn't stretch to a story
with a beginning and ending.
What's more, a winter storm was raging,
drowning out your friendly words.
The wind forced the trees to assume such postures
that even the birds lost all composure.
Relief was written all over their faces
when they could stand up straight again.
And, lastly, for days now, the heating's been seized
with homeric sobs, as though some narrative were imprisoned
inside and were desperate to be released.
A singular dialect only spoken
within the confines of this house.
I'm still working, yes, and can't see myself
breaking off till the curtain.
A while back, I read that philosophers
would be content to merely hit on
one or two new questions—I'm dying
for answers though. The faintest echo
of a single feeble answer
that leaped into my face and stayed there
would be enough.

February '95

At the point where the rivers,
all foam, go crashing into each other,
changing their names,
there is—when the water level's high—
a tiny self-contained pool
that's not worth mentioning:
a child of the thaw.
A quiet resting place
for aquatic birds
that don't seem to know
which flood they
should take to
reach the sea.
For me, with my doubts,
there is a bridge—
a concrete leviathan
which, in a high arc,
is vaulting nature.

Draft of a Nature Poem

1

Twelve sails, spread out across the bay;
your look makes them capsize.

2

A tree stump's testily abuzz
for wasps are plaguing it.

3

Some faithful rain is washing
childhood out of seedcases.

4

Grass is indignant, all greenstuff
is mortified—due to your touch.

5

Heat's building up, indulgent light,
beech trees with ladders down, room where one dies.

6

The book which takes in
and brings forth all looks,
from which we (have to) read each day?

7

And finally: a eulogy on stones.

Postcard from Budapest, April '95

America's burning: the fire's
blue shadow is visible
in every window. A spring
that's prolonging winter
into the impervious world.
April, o lousy muse,
your black tears
are lending ashen luster
to the cobblestones
in the old part of town.
The past is still taking its toll
on Petri, a man with the mottled face
of a hare: a war, he said,
ended here fifty years
back. And Bela is chewing
his hermeneutic beard
and asking: what is our due.
In April, the apples of Budapest
are worm-eaten, sweet.

Summer '95

Swallows are peeling the sky
above the open book:
a peace is being hammered out,
a war declared.
And one stray cloud
is sending its bewildered shadow
wandering across the commands.
Please, declare what war's all about.

Little Scene

The traveler stands there
awaiting the flood tide
with empty hands.
Should he let himself go?
The water arches
like the glass stations
of childhood, a train
has just passed through, and
paper's gavotting above the tracks still—
what's left of a narrow life.
The wave is washing
the pebbles where age
is hurting them most;
they're groaning like an express train
at night, between
ebb and flow.

At Night, beneath Trees

Trees, a loose series,
grouped as though afraid of space
on the downward slope.
One star, already bought from
the mighty skull of Night—
brought by the screech owl.
Words keep faith while things
flood into you;
none betrays you or itself.
Only at the end of this night
spent out under trees
does your mental fog rise
because no questions pester
the answer.

Photo Album

In the same way that fire shoots up out of memory,
setting a childhood alight which was sealed
beneath the firm skin of experience,
the flame of doubt—which can't be put out—
appears in brown photos, begins to lick:
a face swamped with tears starts to hate again
and staggers off on reeling shoulders
as though the only thing that could still save
the precious realm were contorted features.

Note for the Files

At night I again heard
the screams of the birds,
and the grass listened in.
Armistice, loaded
with a live word,
an enduring one. For fifty years
we've been fed by Hitler;
it's time for the others
to eat, and we'll watch
their ugly convulsions,
a fork in each neck.
At night I again heard
the screams of the birds,
the winged epic poem
on *Angst*.

Postcard, in Tiny Writing

for Izet Saraljic

Yesterday we hit a town
you'd think had been gnawed away by wind.
It's on a river that shows us the way
to the enemy. Unaccountably shaped,
this has all the same filth swimming in it
that's filling the deserted streets.
We made our camp in a roof-
less house: and could therefore see
the stars, or what was apparent
in the somber mirror.
A streamlet ran the whole length of our room,
dividing it in two; we drank
until the shit oozed out of our pants.
A doctor came and, unresisting,
we swallowed his pills,
whether poison or not.
"I've spilled all this blood
so the child can breathe in peace"
is a saying in this region,
in which there are said to be bears and wolves.
The people here—still believing
in miracles, shunning the truth—
live off pigeon droppings, the droppings
they sell in the town as dung
for the early vegetables. Money's
in exile. In the last war,
the doctor informed us yesterday,

they buried their enemies up to the waist,
head down, feet up,
so that they looked like a field of vines.
This is the way, if you believe
what he said and fear what he didn't say,
that justice was dispensed in this place.
Both pans of these scales
were chalices brimming over with fresh blood.
I'm fine myself. I'm writing a good deal,
not only letters; the sentences really
flow in the morning, and slow to silence
when dusk approaches. The dark that takes hold then
compels concentration.
No snow's fallen yet. Europe, goodnight.
I'm writing another letter from Mostar,
I hope not the last.

Laughlin's Secret

I must insist on a bed
in this bedlam.
Consider how much
I've suffered in this
best of all worlds.
The name in my identity card
is not mine. No one
knows who I am
(and I won't let on).
It is my secret.
I'd like to see God in this asylum.
I'll tell Him my name.
He'll recognize me straightaway,
will ensure my well-being.

[Eingeborene]

Natives

Just before closedown
a singular people
appeared on the screen. Natives,
the commentator said. They dig
their dead up out of the soil
to kill them a second time
with words—in a lingo
everyone understands
because its rules are arbitrary.
Only thus, said the headman
who'd studied in the West
(as the commentator vouchsafed),
only thus do we have a future:
where others bury their dead
we tear them up out of the earth,
and lick their wounds,
and leave them lying there in the sun.
Then we start out.
In which direction remained unclear
because the little dot supervened,
the flickering green
which wipes out all programs.

Up in the Gods, with Hobbes

for Peter Horst Neumann

Seen from above, where the air is thinner, they're
mushrooms that, though they've just pushed their way through,
are suddenly full-grown, with earth still clogging
their cloddish feet. Art they admire
for there's nothing worth praising any longer.
They tank up on hope. But the melancholy
they're drinking in with bated breath is not easy
to swallow: in every one of those fair, sublime words
a clock is ticking, cleaving the audience's
applause. And later, on leaving, outside the theater,
in the gravelly dark, the visitor comes to see
his clapping was divided: justice,
so his hands drone on, is not a function of goodness.

Education

I'm not one of those
who desired their mother or
longed to kill an intrusive father.
Parental intercourse? Heaven knows,
it was other fantasies which drove me
out of the house. And the burst of light
the comet came with in the night sky
did not seem like an ejaculation.
The rainbow, too, which means so much,
did not join man and woman (or wife)
but heaven and earth.
Yet sometimes I ask myself
whether my ear knows what it's hearing,
my eye what it's seeing.
When I see Mary breast-feeding
her child, I fail to believe
that the body—the talked-to-pieces body—
of Christian culture has
given up its soul. And lastly:
that melancholy dog, my dog,
must not be some kind of subservient son!
Everyone has to come up with something
he or she thinks is true, overtly or covertly,
but there's only one thing which counts in the end:
the inscrutable world.

Trompe l'Oeil

What's beautiful need not be good
and true here on this continent
of ruthlessness where every road
leads into evening, into night.
Look, the barbarians are already
in town, already feel at home.
In their rank gardens, where our weakness
functions as dung, flowers are aspiring
into a world which shuns the light.
They search for warmth as lizards search
to find the sun on baking asphalt.
When your guest's there you mustn't think
a single thing that might displease him,
even if this disillusions the truth.
The truth? All that remains for us
is goodness, hopeless goodness, not
the beautiful, that earning asset,
that power which in our empty faces
runs up the ancient pennant of grief.

Episode

This year too, my friend, there's no way
that joy's about to creep across the globe.
That's what the man next to me in the plane said.
He hailed from east Germany, and was drinking
tomato juice laced with pepper and gin.
And if our suitcase does arrive,
it'll be the last one to whirl round the belt,
and the missus will have made off long before.
A snowstorm drove the plane along in front,
abruptly dropping it so that the map
that bore his name spun down to the floor.
So what? he said, if someone does
find it among the wreckage,
they're only going to hear
"that number's unobtainable."

While Dawn Is Cracking

Falling barometers, rising stock prices,
and what's called life's far out, far out of focus.
Germany, lashed by unrelenting rain,
doubles up, throws a puny sentence out
that's unashamed although the tune is false.
The past has got to end somewhere near here
just like a road that's risen for too long.
What then? A precipice with a sea view?
Or hairpin bends down into the abyss?
Gentlemen dressed in black command the screen,
anxious (before they're pensioned off) to land
a major—no, a stellar—coup, ensuring
that, on the day, their funeral will be broadcast
worldwide. And on the margins of the Conference
for Cooperation on the Decline of Europe,
someone gives voice to hope; the center's silent.
The heavens look most like a monstrous pile
of broken-open mattresses; no wonder
that—once you've dragged yourself from bed—you're glad
when night stops squatting in your dim apartment.

In the Plane, above Europe Still

Far down below, the dark clod that is Europe
breaks up, within spitting distance of the void,
and every still visible thing is trying
to confuse you: tiny cars are gently jogging
along the roads' rusty skeleton,
emitting ever fainter signals of altercations,
catastrophes, whose smoldering fire trail
is veining the scabby body. Water's on the rise.
Asia's little projecting part sinks into the sea
of its scholarly Reason behind the crests
of the clouds, and sends its incomprehensible mutterings
into the hungry dark. A world that's covered with scars
and nodes, an inventory of Beauty.
The sun's now got caught on the uppermost floor
of the Tower of Babel—sizzling noises:
it's burning up all the words left unspoken,
leaving a dinky white flag, unfinished
Hope, all atremble, fluttering on above the rubble.
Smoking's allowed, and a tenuous coffee is being served,
permitting no prophecies. Like a stray dog,
my look goes browsing the tragic chronicle of frontiers,
fading away in the gloaming. In today's paper it says
that at this very moment twelve gentlemen,
sporting collars and ties, are putting their heads to the ground
to pick up an answer to the tautologies
of Freedom: all they hear, though, is the crackling
of the cinders across which the airplane's shadow is flitting.

In Cologne, Winter

The ground in the urban wood is pocked
with tracks. Hoofed beasts, which must have
plodded through andante.
The paper is cheerfully ignorant
although—on the miscellaneous page—
there'd be space enough.
Instead it reports on
a photocopier, new on the market,
which only reproduces the bones
when a hand is laid upon the glass plate.
An osseous skull in one's passport,
and freedom to think up the rest.
The history of evolution
must probably be rewritten
so the end fits.
That is however another story, which—
probably sans memory—
will regale itself with a pretty ending.

Film

I'm looking for nothing. I just see the way
that everything is running backward,
with animals getting bigger,
humans getting smaller—
the way that their dominion wanes.
As though drunk they're stumbling
over signs. This last
great film too,
which shot itself,
is getting very close to the start:
take seven
of every species of beast;
the humans have bowed out already.

In Memory of Cioran

He laughed his fill in the face of Creation.
Every broken stalk was a proof,
every dewdrop a tear,
every letter a bombshell.
Not to even mention Christ,
who loved him like a brother
that has to be sacrificed
to prove one's power.
A kick was the watermark
in his writing, slapstick gags
for ever repeated: for years on end
he shed sleepless tears about Creation,
and now has died peacefully in his sleep.

Rumor, '95

A ghost is abroad
in Germany: it's said
to be small and to speak
in hurt, disabled words
like a foreign child.
And they say it's wearing
a coat, far too big
for its senile body.
And walking in boots,
laced up to the limit,
which tap a shrill rhythm
on cranial sutures—
a rhythm that we're not meant to know.
Does not know its way around,
goes plucking the calendar
with a nimble finger.
Does not know its
name, and laughs
when it sees us—
sees how we are looking at it.
Is not from round here.

The Way They Write

for Paul Wühr

One man raises the stone and writes
a poem on Truth,
which divides and hides.
Another sees the thistle beneath
the stone and only finds words
for grief. From another's fist
the syllables leap. Another screams.
The Alexandrian sits in his archive
and scratches his visage
word by word. Beside him is someone
who's busy composing himself from words;
he's still one line short.
Another is wont to walk through cities,
desperately collecting proof.
Another swaps words
till his face is shining, within
and without. Another discovers a rhyme,
and is tickled black, pleased to death.

Far from Perennial Verses

Far from perennial verses, unaware
of direction and factionless: oblivious,
they follow a path into the dark and suddenly
surface, transformed, in a clearing. They feel no craving
for burnished phrases, neglect to say
what people should do, and what they should not.
And when the Death of God's being mooted,
the Death of Man, they can't be heard.
Plato, Nietzsche, all those poets who fight
fire with fire—so sonority, higher forms, may emerge
from the febrile crepitation—despise
such far from perennial verses. But they still live on
in the lidbeats of the eye which keeps on opening,
closing.

Summer Storm

for Karl Riha

1

. . . and then a wind rose, and squatted down squarely
in the treetops, and played its game
with the leaves: some fell victim immediately
to gravity—as though they'd only been waiting for
permission to fall. Others made use of the updraft
and went drifting off, an alphabet dancing
in ash-gray air. They'd many plans; nostalgia
wasn't their scene at all. A couple of fresher little leaves—
only just unfurled—defied the storm,
clinging like sweet life to branch and trunk.

2

I couldn't help thinking of an empty bookcase,
with just the odd forgotten volume depressing the shelves—
Montale's restrained despair; Lowell's dolphin
(the way it both parts and binds together the ocean); Char's sky,
marbled with gleaming pebbles—
reduced to a flurry of pages
by the wind's inattentive fingers.
Calamity, though it may seem to strike only
us, is older than we are; we're merely
writing some new line (we have to write, to continue its text),
dependable serfs of a script which formed with
the storm, accompanied it. It blew over.

Some distant summer lightning caused the clouds to glow,
and colors—quick as lightning—groped their way back
into things.

3

This scene's been described so often: the lull
that succeeds the storm. Someone says: I prefer
Time to the present, and starts to trudge off.
Another invokes the rustling leaves
and their windy truth beneath blue concrete.
I for my part stand there, feel I'm putting down roots,
beneath bare branches, and fish for the words
that went with the wind, that will come with the wind.

To Zbigniew Herbert

Because a slight, slow-moving brook
often changes out of all recognition
in spring, in the weeks when the thaw sets in,
becoming a prepotent flood which ravishes
both banks while thrusting forcibly through,
there are many, tired of the present, who are now
staring at the dwindling supply of dreams
in the hope that there's something down at the bottom,
a different language underneath language,
enabling one to explain why we feel the urge
to explain (as though enough were not enough).
Not the routine we know as life,
the unfaithful head that's a wide-holed sieve
so we greet the sun each morning
with a fresh "Ah!," a fresh "Oh!"
Many of those who've had a first peep
into the brain conclude that the world is hallucination;
at once they're lost in the Virtual
where trees are only look-alikes.
And on the border?
Stands a mirror the size of the world,
displaying a tree that isn't one:
what used, in our land, to go by the name of reality
can't be distinguished any longer from the illusion
of that reality. Has the world changed
since the man from Media came—or just
our knowledge about the world, the knowledge

which makes it disappear as it goes
its repetitive way? Soon, dear Zbigniew,
we'll cover all this country's mirrors,
and turn all paintings to face the wall,
so the image they throw of us
won't deter the man who eventually
makes for worlds which can't be imagined.

Writers' Congress

Lahti / Finland

Once, surreptitiously, from my window—
in – ex – or – able brightness of the midsummer night—
I listened to the poets discoursing on beauty,
on its insulted truth, on the blotchy lawn
of the hotel. To the small-eyed Russian
who carried his shadow under his arm, as only
a Russian oppressed by the ill will of chalky small hours
can balance a shadow. When words reach us
sleepers, touch shore between two breaths
in morning's soft swell, that mood
of unity/endlessness surfaces,
out of which poems grow like gaunt grass
from crack-filled asphalt. To a sad Swede
who looked like the silent god of identity,
weary of playing with words. Just a breath still,
a syllable, one slight echo in a series of mirrors
which knows no beginning, knows no end.
To a Portuguese woman in flowing shawls
who spoke of the fluttering movements of the female hawk
on being first covered: that's how words conceive
our meaning, like the branch in spring
when penetrated by earth's sap. And finally
to a poet from Poland, with eyes for truth only
(for truth, that's not found in sentences): a man
with dark eyes, who'd got lost in the maze of his melancholy.
To throw light on the predicament of poetry,
he showed the others a coin: no sign

of a head or a tail on that well-worn sphere.
A requiem for the empty space between
spirit and nature underneath a blue-gray sky.
For my part, I (with my head out of sight behind the curtain)
had one or two things on the tip of my tongue regarding the claim
to truth of poetic discourse, but I kept my mouth shut,
and warmed the nascent screams in my mouth
which formed one part of the truth, whose history
is known as sanguinary error. A powerless part—
ransacked, profaned, unable to sew what's been rent
back together. But I couldn't speak, and only saw
my own face in the window's mirror, vague
as molten pitch. And later—it was long
past midnight—a sleep-starved French poet
joined the others. He'd been collecting
pebbles down by the lake in the bright night,
hounded by the rasping cries the seagulls make.
He showed them his trouvailles: we're outside literature
when we talk about it, he said (every word
was audible); we just replicate it, fail
to touch its heart—its hard, indestructible core.
Let us be guests, uninvited but welcome,
fortuitous guests who take a seat
and vanish again without being missed.
The Pole said nothing. The Russian first released his shadow
then skipped after it. The Portuguese woman, wrapped up like a
    mummy,
was probably thinking of the words which celebrate
the body's beauty, unimpressed by death. The Swede
departed smiling like someone who knows
the frailty of what he is doing. I remained standing
behind the window and watched the wind,
which found peace in the bright green of the birch trees.

The Cemetery

Right by the entrance, adjoining the compost heap
where gladioli exhale their stuffy sweetish redness,
a poet I knew well lies buried. He'd brought
a couple of words back from the war
(concealed in a shoe), and these he massaged
till a book took shape: sixty-four pages,
along with an entry—dropped after his death—in the queen
of encyclopedias. His elegiac tone was lauded,
his images, his provenance from Oskar Loerke
(whom he never met). We owe him
spurious rhymes for a spurious life too.
("A herald" was what Benn called him, but the letter's
been lost, so there is no culprit behind
the crime.) Though never monied, he had his muses
who washed his dishes and sent off his poems
while he sprawled, washed-out and sad, on the sofa.
He sensed the stony look that was fixing him
from the future, bleaching his words.
One row behind there's a colleague who, way back in the sixties,
made poetry concrete: God's a word too,
a field day for the atheists.
Long word-chains scattered across the page,
and he the last link, with nowhere to go:
a tidbit for academics, who likened
his poems to sand, to desert, for whatever reason.
He was, when you met him, always returning from a congress
or traveling to a symposium in somewhere like Celle,

strictly second-class, weighed down by lexica
he'd be digging over with sharp fingers, searching
for singular treasures—"oblatio" for "burnt offering,"
you don't understand that you must understand.
He drank himself to death. His name, in lower-case letters,
has lost some characters already:
that would no doubt have pleased him. (An anthology
came out in São Paulo recently, in which he's extolled
as a permanent revolutionary.)
His wife, a more conventional talent, wrote
poems too. In one she compared a person's slowness
with the blinking of an owl. My God,
what vitriol oozed from the critics;
the mildest rebuke was plagiarism.
But whom do words belong to? She's probably
still alive and is washing the blood, with gouty fingers,
from the marble.—Next to the wall that abuts on the road,
awash in the uproar he so often sang of, lies the grave
of the city's sole political poet.
He was a real star, got learned by heart—
each poem he wrote was a tender punch, brief,
dry and telling: the world reveals its set of brown teeth.
He was my neighbor for two years, then he moved to the country
or rather let himself be moved by a woman who nowadays
forges his signature in order to pay the rent.
I couldn't find a grave. And the gardener shook
his head. "A poet? Here? I've no idea
if poets are buried round here, the gravestones
don't tell you, you know." They say he hanged himself.
"Accident" said his family, which could afford
to buy up and stamp out his books of poems.
I was in Rome with him in the eighties:

he fashioned long poems on emperors, popes
and cats in a language so outlandish,
so scintillating, that no one could grasp them. Now
there are some who pride themselves on having always
seen his talent: they praise his high style,
encompassing hatred, beauty and grief in the classical manner,
purifying your vision. I can still hear him laughing,
talking of critics who think that there's progress in poesy,
apart from perceiving the flight of birds that was making its way
from the station toward the Colosseum, where he lived.
Birdflight, script that erases itself . . . No sign of his
grave. And what did that leave? He'd given me
a poem, a pre-text of death, dressed in rhyme,
written in the dark, *in the light from the eyes of a cat*—
it occurred to me then. Outside the cemetery
stood a telephone booth, shining bright; I went inside,
removed the receiver from its cradle and slowly
talked my heart out.

Last Day of the Year

As though the sky were bent on indemnifying the earth,
the rain today has washed all paintings out of frames
which now circumscribe bright patches on the streaky walls.
The world that will come! Only memories keep
their muddy color. The year clogs up in its final hours.
Let nobody say there's plenty of space between cup and lip
when only a handsbreadth separates progress from tripping in
    circles;
the fact is (and this is not a lesson we needed to learn)
that every day a new year begins: the year of war.
It's not an allegory either, like the lounging angel
clamped in a gas mask in smiling galaxies. Now can be heard
the trump which blacks out one-third of the sun,
one-third of the moon, one-third of the stars
without anybody noticing, and—as to the rest—
it implodes like the green dot on TV when the news is over,
the year's last news. And Grace, who loves her enemies too,
has got the date wrong, her deceptive glibness has stut-
tered her into the new year, with the conqueror
reconquered long since: being dragged in chains, for all to see,
across the ocher marketplace of images,
trailing his blood. On the eyes of this dead man
landscapes are growing, an eminent ruin, the rhyming whispering
of the palm trees, a well without words, shaded-in, crosshatched,
captured by our premier painter, who's shyly hiding
behind his camera. Ça va mal, très mal, quoth the demiurge—
he who once again spells what's illegible, makes a fair copy:

obituaries for the eye only. Another hour. It's time
for our foes to show up. *Life's disappeared*
from the earth and is only now to be found in the depths of the ocean.
Was it Kant who saw us surviving on Jupiter?
At any rate, Destiny's off the agenda, we're too deep
in debt, *and the drifting pack ice is spreading,*
spreading farther and farther. Maybe, who knows, this special
moment too was born of a sign from on high—
this second in which we finally pitch down
into silence. I watch the rain; the hedge
the wind's maltreating; the night which, heavy-tongued,
is starting on its salvage work so that the new year
can show its old self.